CLEAN INK

Recovery Poems and Tattoos

CLEAN INK

Recovery Poems and Tattoos

An Anthology
Chosen, Edited, and Contributed by

LINDA PHILLIPS

Threefold Press
Oak Hill, OH, USA
www.3foldpress.com

Clean Ink
© 2022 Linda Phillips
All rights reserved with special permissions for contributing poets and tattoo images.
ISBN 9798437832011

These pages hold a collection of poems dedicated to those affected by addiction and those working on their recovery, showing others the way out.

We see you.

"If we are painstaking about this phase of our development, we will be amazed before we are halfway through. We are going to know a new freedom and a new happiness. We will not regret the past nor wish to shut the door on it. We will comprehend the word serenity and we will know peace."

Promises of Alcoholics Anonymous
Pages 83-84 in The Big Book

Contents

Free Verse

Lost Time
Amber Richards (Ohio, USA) 3

Life Lessons
Amber Richards (Ohio, USA) 4

To Dad
Amber Richards (Ohio, USA) 5

Addiction
Johnathon Eyler (Ohio, USA) 6

Pull
Elizabeth S. (Ohio, USA) 7

Time
Shannon Rae Elliott (Ohio, USA) 8

Dust in the Wind
Peggy Robinson (Ohio, USA) 9

Battlefield
Amanda Willcoxen (Ohio, USA) 10

Free Verse Continued

I'll Show You
Natasha Gray (West Virgina, USA) 11

Final Goodbye
Michelle Chasteen (Ohio, USA) 12

A Pretty Little Lady
Michelle Chasteen (Ohio, US) 13-14

The Call
Jennifer Morris (Ohio, USA) 15

Christmas Music
Marzella DePasquale (Ohio, USA) 16

Experience, Strength, and Hope
Lori Williams (Ohio, USA) 17

Ready
Margo Smith (Ohio, USA) 18

Dopeless Hopefiend
Gwen Grimes (Ohio, USA) 19-20

One More Goodbye
Ekari Marevoni (Lilongwe, Malawi) 21

On My Way- The Goodbye Letter
Linda LaForge (Michigan, USA) 22-23

Free Verse Continued

Happy Mirage
Linda Phillips (Ohio, USA) 24

Be Still and Know
Linda Phillips (Ohio, USA) 25

Security Check
Linda Phillips (Ohio, USA) 26

Hope
Tiffany Royster (Ohio, USA) 27

Is There A.. -15062021
Michael Crooijmans (Arnhem, The Netherlands) 28-29

Pangs of New Hope
Joel Oyeleke Ifeoluwa (Port Harcourt, Nigeria) 30

Final Call
Roy K. (Washington, USA) 31-33

Tattoos

Ronnie Hicks (Pennsylvania, USA) 37
Jessika R. (Ohio, USA) 38
Lauren McFadden (Ohio, USA) 39
Rhonda Johnson (Ohio, USA) 40

Tattoos Continued

Allison Gutierrez/ Derek Oyer (Ohio, USA) 41
Brad Clabaugh (Ohio, USA) 42
Toni Schmidt (Michigan, USA) 43
Daphne Long (Ohio, USA) 44
Kristina Camden (Ohio, USA) 45
Erik Miller (Ohio, USA) 46-47

Acrostic

TRIALS
Elizabeth S. (Ohio, USA) 51

LYRIC
Amanda Willcoxen (Ohio, USA) 52

LEARN
Natasha Gray (West Virgina, USA) 53

STABLE
Paula Robinson (Ohio, USA) 54

WAIT
Linda Phillips (Ohio, USA) 55

RALLY
Linda Phillips (Ohio, USA) 56

CLEAN
Andrea C. (Ohio, USA) 57

Haiku * Senyru * Tanka

natural beauty
Laughing Waters (Alabama, USA) 61

poppyhead
Laughing Waters (Alabama, USA) 62

wide open iris
Laughing Waters (Alabama, USA) 63

sunset flames
Laughing Waters (Alabama, USA) 64

handcrafted cross
Laughing Waters (Alabama, USA) 65

poppies petals
Laughing Waters (Alabama, USA) 66

tarnished coins
Laughing Waters (Alabama, USA) 67

gambler's game over
Laughing Waters (Alabama, USA) 68

silent wind chimes
Laughing Waters (Alabama, USA) 69

memories leaving
Laughing Waters (Alabama, USA) 70

Haiku * Senyru * Tanka Continued

cradling
Laughing Waters (Alabama, USA) 71

paper birds
Laughing Waters (Alabama, USA) 72

wake up
Natasha Pleasant (Ohio, USA) 73

your warmth, my wish
Natasha Gray (West Virginia, USA) 74

of the spell
Linda Phillips (Ohio, USA) 75

corrupted logic
Linda Phillips (Ohio, USA) 76

do-over
Linda Phillips (Ohio, USA) 77

birth day
Linda Phillips (Ohio, USA) 78

blind
Linda Phillips (Ohio, USA) 79

Haiku * Senyru * Tanka Continued

hullabaloo chase
Linda Phillips (Ohio, USA) 80

florescent rainbows
Amanda-Jane Bayliss (West Yorkshire, England) 81

new beginnings
Michelle Chasteen (Ohio, USA) 82

together again
Lori Williams (Ohio, USA) 83

as the leaves fall
Angela Ward (Ohio, USA) 84

freedom
Caitlin Adkins (Ohio, USA) 85

when the rain falls
Paula Robinson (Ohio, USA) 86

anew
Elizabeth S. (Ohio, USA) 87

How you can help 89

FORWARD

It is said that music is the message of the soul. Music is various forms of poetry with a catchy tune added. Poetry and tattoos are beautiful messages expressing an inward struggle, battle, war, victory, praise, joy, hurt, and healing. Life can be painful. That is real.

I have been personally immersed in the world of addiction through fighting the battle with my daughter, as a recovery group leader, and as CEO of the Field of Hope outreach. Those who fall into the trap of substance abuse are just like us. We have other cracks in our armor that people can't see. In the Bible, Romans 3 says that as members of the human race, we *all* fall short of the glory of God.

I am excited about Linda's work in sharing the real lives of those traveling from addition to recovery with others. May each one sharing know they are shining a light onto another person's path in recovery and becoming part of their victory story.

"Love God and love others – the two greatest things you can do"
-Jesus Christ

Kevin Dennis

PREFACE

Everyone who struggles with addiction has a story. To speak your story is one thing; to *feel* and *process* it through the written word is another. Much scientific proof, including evidence-based articles like "Emotional and Physical Health Benefits of Expressive Writing," published online by Cambridge University Press on January 2, 2018, recommends writing as a pivotal form of processing thoughts and information.

Having experienced addiction myself and with family members, writing has proven a therapeutic outlet for me over the years. My title as Program Director and Substance Abuse Counselor at the Field of Hope Community Campus has provided me with the opportunity to offer our clients the same tools.

I was privileged to witness these women's transformation within one group writing session. Most did not recognize themselves as poets at all, and within an hour, the entire group left feeling more creative and capable of more than they could have imagined. THAT is what it is all about for me.

Recovery tattoos are an outlet for many individuals in recovery. Worn as a badge of honor, recovery tattoos represent the battles faced in addiction and encourage continued sobriety. Lauren McFadden, a contributor to this anthology, shared, "My tattoo reminds me of the promises of recovery. It encourages me always to keep my faith in God, and He will never let me fall, as long as I stay near to Him." The emotional connection to one's recovery tattoo cannot be ignored and proved to be a beautiful companion to the poems in this anthology.

In 2021, Field of Hope Community Campus began a mental health program with the plan to implement art therapy. This vision prompted the *Clean Ink* poetry anthology project, where 50% of the proceeds will provide the materials needed to facilitate these groups.

Although most entries were locally submitted from Gallia County, Ohio, home of the Field of Hope Community Campus; there were worldwide submissions to the *Clean Ink* project. I hope each poem and recovery tattoo message reaches your heart as they have all done mine.

Linda Phillips

ACKNOWLEDGMENTS

My life, family, career path, this project, and the projects to come would not be possible without Jesus, His protection, and His grace in placing the following key players in my recovery and life journey.

In remembrance of my sponsor, Halli M., who left this earth too soon. She loved me until I could love myself. Willie N., for being my surrogate grandfather and forever giving me snapping turtle stories. We will have some catching up to do when I get to heaven. Deb K., for always telling me how it is and showing me that it is okay to be real. You are the real deal.

I want to thank my family who sacrificed their time with me, so completing this project would be possible. I could not have done it without your support.

I am grateful to Amber Richards and Kevin Dennis for believing in this project and me. As bold visionaries, you pave the road for myself and others to believe anything is possible when God is in it.

Thank you to those who put their hearts to paper and entrusted me with your message. It brings joy to my spirit to bring this book to you.

-Linda

Chapter One
Free Verse

Lost Time
by Amber Richards

As I sit and look at my little girl's beautiful face, it takes me back to that wonderful place

Me and her skipping and walking hand in hand, or just playing, building castles in the sand

As I sit in prison and think of how she has grown, it reminds me of those opportunities with her I have blown

Her being so young and asking where mommy went makes me realize that instead of chasing drugs, my time with her I should have spent

God is teaching me what I need to know
about how to stay clean, be a good mother, and every day I grow

The game I played, I was never ahead, but God sent me here, so I didn't wind up dead

The game was at first all right, and I thought it was fun, but at the end, when it's got you, you do nothing but run

I want to put all of it in my past and lay down peacefully with my little angel at last

Life Lessons
by Amber Richards

I'm sitting in this prison watching days go by, thinking about all my mistakes of getting high

Thanking God for my struggles, battles, and strife, because my being here has saved my life

There are so many lessons here for me to learn, and so many bridges at home I must burn

I went through all this for a reason, I know God wants me to show others a new season

Not knowing what He has in store,
just knowing He is always at my door

Hurts, habits, and hang-ups can get us all, maybe I can help by telling others what I saw

No one wants to come to this lonely place, it has shoved reality right in my face

To Dad
by Amber Richards

I look at you and I see,
what a true father is supposed to be
I miss all our fun times playing ball,
you are always picking me up when I fall
I'm sorry for everything that I put you through
This time here is changing me and making me new
You have always shown me unconditional love
Just like my heavenly father up above

Addiction
by Johnathon Eyler

Hello. I'm Addiction, I'm your new best friend
I'll be there when nobody else will, I'll be there 'til the end

The first time that we met, I got you high as high could be
I was all you could think about, I made you feel so free

I make you forget about all the pain and the past
Each time we get together, it just may be our last

Each time it's more than the first time, you can't get enough, you want more
The next thing you know, you pass out and end up on the floor

You feel trapped in this relationship, you want to run and flee
You've tried 12 Steps, but you stumble just after Step 3

It takes just one step and all this you will see
HIS NAME IS JESUS CHRIST, HE CAME TO SET YOU FREE.

Pull
by Elizabeth S.

You were so attractive to me
    Irresistible at one point
Controlling thoughts every day
    As if I ever had a choice

The farther from you I am
    The stronger I get
Sometimes you still whisper in my ear
    But I won't give up yet

Time
by Shannon Rae Elliott

If I could turn back time, I think I would wait for it to open a brand new gate

The struggles I have been through and the things I have seen I wouldn't take back because it makes me, me

I thought I knew what pain was tho; I only got a taste until I saw the tears run down my kid's face

I will never go back to that; I have learned from my mistakes; I will never make a broken promise to ruin my kid's faith

I am saying goodbye to my past and hello to my future 'cause God has created in me a new creature

Dust in the Wind
by Peggy Robinson

We are dust in the wind
        Here today, gone tomorrow
                You are the apple of my eye
                        I will not take life for granted

Battlefield
by Amanda Willcoxen

The time has finally arrived,
it's a feeling that can't be described
Life is definitely worth living
I'm going to take a little less and do more giving

Recovery is the key to my survival,
along with Jesus and reading my Bible
All it takes sometimes is a little grace,
because the hurt and pain can't be erased

The substances just put them on hold
until the moment you lose all control
You feel like your whole world is caving in, but let me tell you,
THIS is a battle you can win

I'll Show You
by Natasha Gray

I've been fat, I've been thin
I've done anything to fit in

All the pain, all the hurt
All the things that never work

I've tried to run, I've tried to hide
I've pushed it until I died

All the progress, all the change
All the times I've turned the page

I've made my choice; I've begun something new
I'm going to show you what I can do!

Final Goodbye
by Michelle Chasteen

The vicious cycle of chaos and nightmares is coming to an end
I'm finally capable of saying goodbye to what I thought was my only friend

No more do I have to battle with sin
No more testing and teasing the devil to see if I can win

I have hope and faith today
The old me has begun to decay

It's time for me to blossom and bloom
No more do I have to sit in doom

It's time for the new me to break free!

So, today I say my final goodbye to you
Because this warrior just ain't got it to do

A Pretty Little Lady
by Michelle Chasteen

A pretty little lady, playin' with sin
Dancing with the devil to see if she could win

Lost her pride, covered with a mask
A shield of armor from everyone with a task

Putting on a smile but screaming inside
"Can you hear me?" she often cried

Roaming the streets lost, but prayed to be found
Crawling in a corner, trying to drown out the sound

While looking in the mirror, the tears just came
Stealing, cheating, and lying are the name of the game

How do I get out of here? Can I go home?
I know mama is waiting, but the streets are where I roam

I can hear the streets calling; they scream my name
The circus in my head is making me insane

I don't want these feelings; I want happiness inside
How do I get off this long bumpy ride?

Then there they were, reaching for my hand
"Come with us," they said, "We understand."

It was long, hard work, but the pain went away
I started to smile, then started to pray

God led me where I have meant to go
I just had a few curveballs, and my timing was slow

I know now where I've been
And what to do, not to go there again

Mama is not crying, and my babies are fed
I now have somewhere comfortable to lay my head

So I will keep saying my prayers and never look back
Counting my lucky stars, my life is on track

The Call
by Jennifer Morris

Not really knowing how to calm the storm I felt within
My life was plagued by addictions, mistakes, and sin

Feelings of emptiness and contempt filled my now broken heart
Knowing what I had to do but no willingness to start

A battle between the devil and angel whispering in my ear
As one gave me hope, the other filled my head with fear

I fell on my knees and cried out to God in utter despair
"I can't do this alone, and You are the only one who's there!"

Later that day, I made a call
to a place I heard that can help you up when you fall

God led me to the door; I was weary and scared
They took me in with open arms and showed me they cared

My head is now clear, and my hands no longer shake
Making that call was the best decision I could make

Christmas Music
by Marzella DePasquale

Crisp cool air

                      Snowflakes falling

                                        Crackle of the fire

              Family gathered 'round

Chatter of the kids

                                Oh! How I love that sound

Experience, Strength, and Hope
by Lori Williams

Experience has brought me here
As my eyes begin to tear,
I remember the pain year after year
God is with me always; I have nothing to fear

My strength gave me the will
The Holy Spirit, He will fill
Now I have the desire
He is still fanning the fire

I believe there is hope
I'm finally off the dope
It's been quite a while,
but now I wear a smile

Ready
by Margo Smith

I've caused loved ones a lot of pain
Have I caused too much destruction,
leaving no more trust available to gain?
Fear of time that has been lost
Memories were made without me there
Too many years have come and gone
while I was too high to notice or care
And though it seems a bit crazy
I am so afraid of letting go
The addict that has been within me
is the only person left I know
How do I say goodbye to this life?
I've lived unhealthy for many years
Now here I sit trying to start new
How could I not be full of all this fear?
For most of my adult life
I viewed the world through my addictive sight
I was scared of life in sobriety
Fearing I'd never get it right
But I'm gonna try this one last time
I'm gonna give it all I have to give
I'm ready to stop running from fear,
so that I can finally move forward and LIVE!

Dopeless Hopefiend
by Gwen Grimes

Mind racin', steady pacin' the floor, down to my last tenth wonderin', how I'm gonna get more

I'm a hopeless dopefiend, can't you see?

Don't care about you or your family, only me!

I will wipe you clear of every dime, speakin' of which, let me do mine

I let the devil inside; it's he who I cannot deny

Soulless, lifeless, hopeless is what you'll find when you look into my worn-out eyes

Devil tried to end my life not once, not twice, but nine times

I had that feeling of utter defeat, but I wised up and laid it all at

God's feet, where He breathed new life into me.

My God is a jealous God who didn't let the devil win; it is Him and me in this fight until the very end

I once was blind, but now I see -viewing life through new clarity

I've had a vision of hope, and I no longer need dope to survive; all it takes is the willingness to start and accept Jesus Christ into your heart

You then too can be like me, living as a Dopeless Hopefiend!

One More Goodbye
by Ekari Marevoni

One more goodbye and I am done
I've been fighting a nasty addiction
It feels like I am its puppet
I hate the feeling of regret right after
I always tell myself this is the last time
Just one more goodbye and I am done

One more goodbye and I am done
I've been crying a lot, trying to make myself brave after
I tell myself this is the last time I will cry about this
Just one more time crying my heart out
One more goodbye and I am done

One more goodbye and I am done
Telling it to my impatience,
"Try to be still; please try one more week,"
But do I have to do it now, maybe next time
One more goodbye and I am done

One more goodbye and I am done
It's hard to give up what you enjoy
One more goodbye is a song without an end
You have to remember what it cost you before singing it
I am done

On My Way- The Goodbye Letter
by Linda LaForge

Now it's time to say goodbye
To all the bull-crap, shame, and lies
No longer will it be my nature
For blackouts to become my major

Goodbye Jose', Jim, and Jack
For certainly I won't be back
Do not call, do not write
I do not care to see your site

No longer will you make me sick
Advise bad choices for me to pick
No longer will you make me cry
Advising me to tell those lies

Goodbye my powder-friend, Cocaine
And to you too, Mary-Jane
You've been there to enhance my speed
And for being my sleepy weed

I say, "No more!" to you two
That I can spend my time with you
No longer will you haunt my brain
No longer will I be insane

Now it's time to say goodbye
And cut off ALL our friendly ties
No longer will you be for me
I'm on my way to recovery

Happy Mirage
by Linda Phillips

Do what makes you happy
    Perception at an age
Life with this philosophy
    Can put you in a cage

Do what makes you happy
    Feelings over truth
Consequences coming
    Treading on our youth

Do what makes you happy
    Seems innocent enough
But I've never found true happiness
    Until I called life's bluff

Be Still and Know
by Linda Phillips

Become still and know

Know

and become

Become in the unmoving silence

Fear will flee

Become in the vacant thoughts

Despair will dissolve

Become in the peaceful nothing

Shame will subdue

Be still and know

Know

and be

Security Check
by Linda Phillips

confused by the message
blind
scared to see
what's lurking behind
who
I've been programmed
to be
allowing others
to wire this mess
left wary answers
to life's difficult test
bogus deposits
made
without care-
vampires who left me
to drown in despair
the burn of betrayal
and no longer safe
left every intent
to be checked
at the gate

Hope
by Tiffany Royster

Feeling helpless and fear
Is the end to this hell near?

In the night, crying and alone
Praying God will get me out of this black hole

Falling to sleep with the demons still laughing
Waking up to a phone call to freedom; thanking God for answering

Off to a new start with my answered prayer
Now nothing but love and hope without fear

Is there a ... - 15062021
by Michael Crooijmans

Is there a future
Without dependency
Is there a future
Without the lasting pain
Of fear, subjugation
And insecurity
Is there a future
Within my reach
And emotional availability
That lies ahead
Where true romance
Leaves me speechless
Within the beauty of dignity
Will I maintain my truest spirit
The beauty of art
Only to feel ashamed and lost
And turned into stone
The damage, guilt, the shame
My heart in pieces, severed
Walking alone
It inflicts, numbs
And misdirects
When it leads you away
From home
Unsure of the loss to overcome

To lose oneself
For all that it affects
It awaits you by scope
Tell me, honestly, dear
Can you tell me how you feel
Are you ok
Are you doing well
Also without the hurt
And without the ecstasy

In a future where one can finally heal

Pangs of New Hope
by Joel Oyeleke Ifeoluwa

A light has been lit up in our path
We have left the wrong way and turned to the right path
The habits that struck us and made us miserable
Is no longer in our life, eligible

The pangs of new hope
That we all want rather than dope
Hope from a life of sorrows and torment
Hope from a life of being wanted by the government

In the saga, we have all experienced
We have finally let go of all the
Bad habits we were once consistent under its influence
Now shining bright in our eyes
Pangs of new hope for a better life do rise

We would no longer indulge in any activity
That would make our recovery status a mere nonentity
We are changed for the better
And of course, we must wear the PANGS OF NEW HOPE like
a sweater

Final Call
by Roy K.

he awoke
thankfully where he
fell asleep...
passed out... again
shook the empty cans

showered
slept some more
choices
he's thirsty again
for another night

which seem to end badly
he chose to walk
out the door
up to the chevron station
sighs

forgot his wallet
next door
AA meeting
changed his choice
walked in and grabbed coffee

he decided to stay
to stay
for awhile
everyday
days turned

into weeks
then months
to a year
new friends
a new mindset

sunset orange
sky explodes off
ocean waves
the rhythm at dawn
he will enjoy it too

the bottle gone
healing begins
serenity courage
wisdom
powerless over alcohol

a quitter
yet in the long run
he won
so he stays
for a while longer

the ebb and flow
of a new song drifts
shine on

Ocean waves sweep the shore
daily reminder that
he has another day
sober
last call

became final call

Chapter Two
Tattoos

Photo credit and tattoo by Ronnie Hicks- Butler, PA
"Alcoholics Anonymous Sobriety Circle and Triangle"

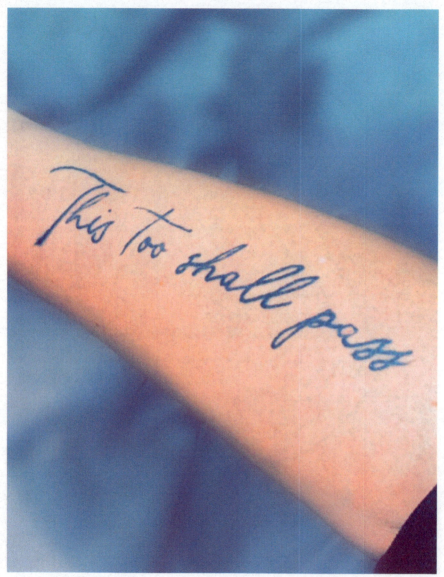

Photo submitted by Jessika R. - Sylvania, Ohio

Photo submitted by Lauren McFadden- Portsmouth, Ohio

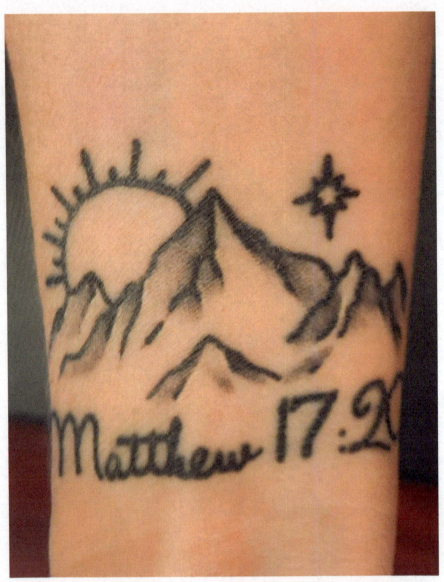

Photo submitted by Rhonda Johnson- Bidwell, Ohio

Photo submitted by Allison Gutierrez. She shares a special moment supporting her brother, Derek Oyer, who is in recovery and currently an addiction counselor for the counseling center, Warriors 4 Christ. - Jackson, Ohio

"There is hope should oceans rise or mountains fall. He never fails."

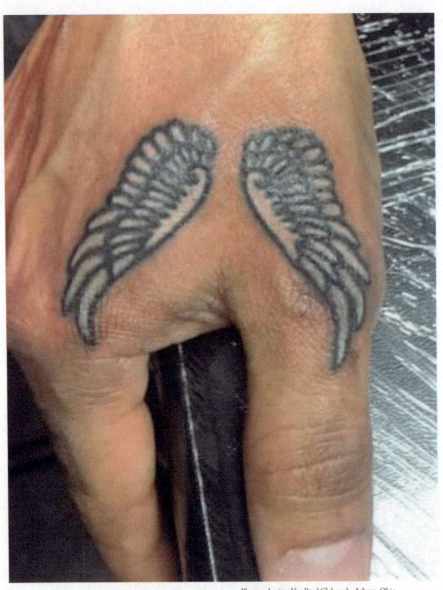

Photo submitted by Brad Clabaugh- Athens, Ohio
"AA Wings"

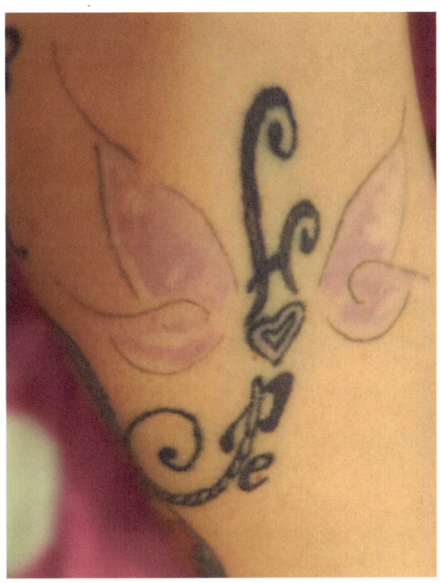

Photo submitted by Toni Schmidt- Alpena, Michigan

Photo submitted by Daphne Long- Gallipolis, Ohio

Photo submitted by Kristina Camden- Wheelersburg, Ohio

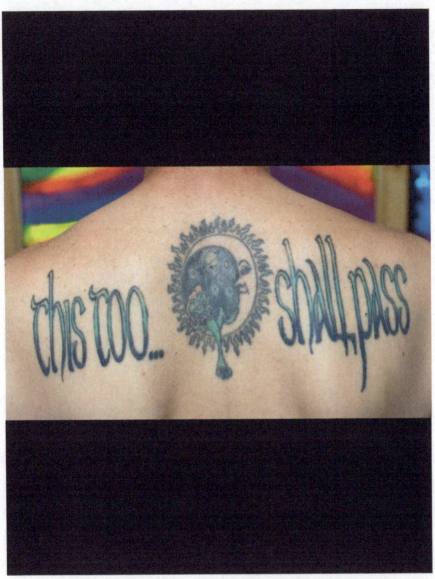

Photo submitted by Erik Miller- Gallipolis, Ohio

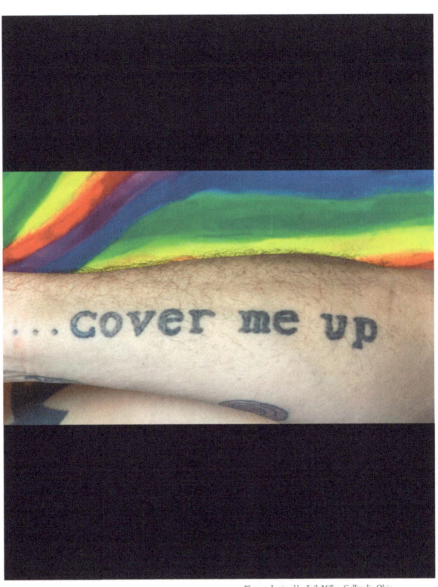

Photo submitted by Erik Miller- Gallipolis, Ohio
Inspired by the Jason Isbell song, "Cover Me Up."

Chapter Three
Acrostic

TRIALS
by Elizabeth S.

T *ransformation or temptation?*

R *eality or regret?*

I *nsight or impasse?*

A *cceptance or ailment?*

L *esson or loss?*

S *uccess or sabotage?*

LYRIC
by Amanda Willcoxen

L *isten with*

Y *our heart and*

R *ealize that*

I *nside of you*

C *ontains a beautiful song*

LEARN
by Natasha Gray

L *ean on others*

E *verything is an opportunity*

A *ppreciate mistakes*

R *emember*

N *ever give up*

STABLE
by Paula Robinson

S *tarting over*

T *rusting God*

A *ffliction ended*

B *earing the pain*

L *osing the fear*

E *verything restored*

WAIT
by Linda Phillips

W *ondering not if, but when*

A *lways hypervigalent*

I *t is never as it seems*

T *omorrow may be the day*

RALLY
by Linda Phillips

R *aise up an army where radical love*

A *lways wins and*

L *oose lip mockers*

L *ay silenced and where I am*

Y *oked for victory*

CLEAN
by Andrea C.

Since I have been clean, I have been

C *ourageous*

L *oving*

E *nthusiastic*

A *mazing*

N *onviolent*

Chapter Four
Haiku * Senyru * Tanka

natural beauty
capture my eyes
it was so sad --
her irises blooming
faded poppies

by Laughing Waters

poppyhead
sleepy dew
in his veins
wild mustang
running into the sunset

by Laughing Waters

wide open iris...
milkweed dew
on the silenced lips
unanswered question
was it the end or beginning

by Laughing Waters

sunset flames...
poppies flickering
in the breeze
from the passing by cars
I count my blessings

by Laughing Waters

handcrafted cross
on the poppy head
mothers milk tears

by Laughing Waters

poppies petals
burning
sundown tones

by Laughing Waters

tarnished coins
on my eyes --
Gods hand

by Laughing Waters

gambler's game over ...
thanks for playing
God

by Laughing Waters

silent wind chimes
dividing now & then
paper cranes

by Laughing Waters

memories leaving
the paper cranes room
silent footsteps

by Laughing Waters

cradling
an unfinished paper crane
her tiny hands

by Laughing Waters

paper birds
beating against
the draped mirror

by Laughing Waters

No way out, it seems
If only you were aware
Of the grace you carry
From our faithful and kind God
There is undying strength in you

by Natasha Pleasant

Your warmth, my wish
The impulse; the yearning
What a vicious end

by Natasha Gray

of the spell earth cast
struggling against time to
resolve meaning

by Linda Phillips

corrupted logic
hearts pierced, perception drives the
tears to the same end

by Linda Phillips

It is never too late
Waves wipe sand in the hot sun
The slate is now clean

by Linda Phillips

How did we get here
Glares from nurses- wires- beep
Shaking little toes

by Linda Phillips

blind to the patterns
catbird perched in leafless trees
mewing her forecast

by Linda Phillips

hullabaloo chase
challenges simple desire
to be left alone

by Linda Phillips

Florescent rainbows
Acres of strawberry fields
Rebirthed second chance

by Amanda-Jane Bayliss

My changing seasons
The heart, mind, body, and soul
Refresh, take a breath
Release all that holds me back
New Beginnings come my way

by Michelle Chasteen

Together again
Resilient strong determined
Souls reunited

by Lori Williams

As the leaves fall off
thank you, God, for one more day
a change is made

by Angela Ward

Sunshine beating down
Smell of fresh air-
Joy of freedom!

by Caitlin Adkins

When the rain falls hard
Everything begins again
A fresh start once more

by Paula Robinson

A flower blooms now
Over a patch of plain grass
Growth is beautiful

by Elizabeth S.

Thank You

Thank you for supporting our recovery efforts.

Help others on the path of recovery by leaving a book review at **www.amazon.com**.

Follow Our Journey

You can follow Field of Hope Community Campus on all major media platforms: Twitter, Facebook, Instagram, and Tik Tok.

To donate or find out more about our programs, visit **www.fieldofhope.life**

Made in the USA
Columbia, SC
18 April 2022